BOOK ANALYSIS

Written by Delphine Leloup
and Lucile Lhoste
Translated by Carly Probert
and Emma Hanna

Brave New World
BY ALDOUS HUXLEY

Bright
≡Summaries.com

ALDOUS HUXLEY

BRITISH WRITER

- **Born in Godalming (Surrey) in 1894.**
- **Died in Los Angeles in 1963.**
- **Notable works:**
  - *Music at Night* (1931), essay collection
  - *Brave New World* (1932), novel
  - *Island* (1962), novel

Aldous Huxley was born in 1894 and was a politically engaged English writer. He was familiar with the major totalitarian regimes of the 20th century and the social tensions that arose from them. When his eyesight began to fail in 1914 he was discharged from the army and was able to devote himself to his academic studies, particularly in English literature, which he studied at Oxford.

His first published novel, *Chrome Yellow*, appeared in 1921, and his most successful work was *Brave New World*, which was published in 1932. Huxley was known for his habit of writing under the influence of various illicit substances, and due to his blindness it can be reasonably assumed that his books were written with the help of assistants. He died in 1963 in Los Angeles.

BRAVE NEW WORLD

A FUTURISTIC SOCIETY

- **Genre:** science fiction novel
- **Reference edition:** Huxley, A. (2007) *Brave New World*. London: Vintage.
- **1st edition:** 1932
- **Themes:** conditioning, consumerism, individualism, technology, freedom, eugenics

Brave New World is a science fiction novel which was published in 1932. It depicts a "perfect" world, where each individual belongs to a specific social class that determines their needs and prospects. Even though this way of life deprives them of their freedom, they have been conditioned to accept it as normal from a very young age.

Throughout the novel, Huxley warns against the vices of Western society, where consumerism and individualism are rampant and technology is ever-more important. Dystopian narratives were also used by other contemporary writers such

as George Orwell (1903-1950) in *1984* (1949) and
Animal Farm (1945).

SUMMARY

THE VISIT

Brave New World is set in the World State, where individuals are divided into different social classes named Alpha, Beta, Gamma, Delta and Epsilon, each of which is sub-divided into "Pluses" and "Minuses". Each of these classes has a different function, ranging from intellectualism in the Alpha class to the manual labour performed by the Epsilons. Each class is educated in a way that preserves this system.

A number of young new recruits are given a tour of the Central London Hatchery and Conditioning Centre by the Director of Hatcheries and Conditioning (DHC), who explains these concepts to them and alludes to some of the unpublished scientific experiments carried out there. The DHC leads a team of researchers who aim to create a utopian society by monitoring and controlling the next generation of children before they are even born.

The rest of the visit is conducted by a researcher called Mr Foster, who explains the different steps in the process used to create human beings. They stop at an incubator, where infants are undergoing tests that will determine their future passions. The students then meet Mustapha Mond, one of the ten "World Controllers", who reminds them of the benefits of a life that has no attachments to any family or household.

Meanwhile, during a conversation with one of her colleagues, Lenina Crowne admits that she wants to be faithful to Henry Foster. However, monogamy is proscribed by the regime. They then discuss Bernard Marx, a grumpy idealist whom Lenina seems to be attracted to. Having agreed to meet her, Marx visits his friend Helmholtz Watson and they discuss their desire for freedom of expression. Meanwhile, Lenina visits Henry Foster and spends some time with him. Marx goes to a Solidarity Service to commune with others, where he takes *soma*, a powerful drug which puts him in a kind of trance. Although this session is supposed to bring him happiness, it has no lasting effect on him.

THE "SAVAGE"

Shortly afterwards, Marx goes on holiday with Lenina and tries to make her more conscious of the conditioning they are subjected to. She is embarrassed, and persuades him to take drugs to forget his loneliness. They then visit the Savage Reservation in New Mexico, where the couple meet John and his mother, Linda, a former Beta-Minus who got lost in the area a few years earlier during a hike with the DHC. Linda has raised her son to understand civilised culture and has taught him to read.

This has given John a keen interest in the world of technology, and Marx decides that it would be interesting to help him discover it. John accepts, not suspecting that this new world will lead to his doom. After leaving to obtain passes, Marx returns to the Reservation to find his new ward. Back at the Conditioning Centre, when he is about to be fired by the DHC, Marx presents Linda and John to the public. They both address the Director, who is John's father, leaving him racked with humiliation; he then leaves the room and immediately resigns.

As the guardian of the "Savage", Bernard is now in a privileged social position: women flock to see him, he throws parties and is catapulted to fame. But John begins to notice the way that this society is mistreating his mother, who has now been drugged with *soma*. He becomes increasingly interested in Lenina and starts trying to keep his distance from both her and the public eye, which puts paid to Bernard's dreams of glory. Lenina, who returns John's feelings, goes to find him in the hope of seducing him, but she is unexpectedly rejected by him, as he is actually only in love with an idealised version of her he has created in his own mind, which would be shattered if they had sex.

Later, we discover that Linda is dying. John visits her in hospital, where his public display of grief is considered shameful by the nurses and the children in the ward. After his mother's death, John decides to raise awareness about the consequences of overdosing on *soma*. Unfortunately, society has been subjected to such heavy conditioning that the people do not understand the ramifications of his speech.

JUDGEMENT

Later, John, Watson and Bernard are arrested by the militia and taken to face judgement for failing to integrate into the system. After a long debate about the "brave new world" and the soundness of its principles, Mustapha Mond decides the three defendants' fates. Since Bernard Marx is an outcast, he is sent to Iceland, where his inner self will be able to flourish and he will live with a population of like-minded individuals; this is not so much a punishment as it is an opportunity for him to adopt a lifestyle that suits his personality. Watson receives the same sentence, and is forced into exile on the Falkland Islands. John wants to join them, but Mond decrees that he must remain, as he is curious to see how his integration into society will progress.

During his speech, Mond admits that he is fully aware that the principles of the World State suppress individual and collective freedoms, because these principles cannot be questioned. He shows tolerance and understanding towards the three rebels, and starts a discussion with John about God; he even eventually offers John a number of books from the former regime which have been banned.

John longs for more privacy and therefore moves into a lighthouse, where he is regularly harassed by journalists and visitors who watch him as if he were an animal in a zoo. He is tormented by guilt over the way he has turned his back on his own principles to live in this new world and by his love for Lenina, which even leads him to start self-harming. Eventually, his irrepressible sexual urges and his inability to find inner peace drive him mad, and he decides to end his life by hanging himself.

CHARACTER STUDY

BERNARD MARX

Bernard Marx is a member of the Alpha class and works for the Psychology Bureau. He is described as an ugly man who is much shorter than most of the other Alpha citizens, which is the result of an anomaly during his conception. In this society, a variety of substances are injected into the uterus during gestation; for example, foetuses which will belong to the Gamma class are injected with alcohol to stunt their growth, and there is a rumour that Bernard received this treatment by mistake. For this reason, he hates working with Gamma citizens because he is afraid of being mistaken for one of them, since they look so similar (see Chapter 4).

He has a fairly poor reputation among his colleagues. After he meets John, his personality and outlook begin to change.

Before he meets John

Bernard suffers from an inferiority complex and is something of an outcast. He is a romantic at heart, and finds it difficult to accept the sexual freedom of the "brave new world", where men and women alike are reduced to mere sexual objects (see Chapter 3). He is quite rebellious, and disagrees with the way the world he lives in is governed. He finds his work on hypnopaedia (sleep-learning) in young children restrictive and utterly useless. His peers often mistake his world-weariness for grumpiness, and his inability to fit in because of his differences is a source of great chagrin for him.

After he meets John

Marx becomes very popular after he returns from the Reservation. He gains a certain degree of power from his position as John's guardian, as everyone who wants to see him must go through Bernard. His self-confidence begins to grow, and his arrogance drives away his friends Helmholtz and John, who feel maligned and used, respectively. However, his time in the spotlight is fleeting and he is soon plunged back into obscurity.

During certain scenes, such as his arrest and trial, he is shown to be a coward, and he even tries to use Linda to appeal a sanction that was imposed on him by the DHC by convincing her to reveal that the DHC is John's father and exposing him to public ridicule. However, he is unable to escape being sentenced to exile in Iceland, even though he has been striving to avoid this fate for a long time, and is forced to say his goodbyes to John and Watson.

HELMHOLTZ WATSON

Helmholtz Watson is an Alpha citizen who works for the College of Emotional Engineering as an Alpha-Plus lecturer. He also sometimes writes for a radio magazine on the side, and he has a gift for writing hypnopaedic slogans. He is passionate about poetry.

Watson is a tall, burly man with very broad shoulders. He has curly black hair and chiselled facial features; in other words, he is as handsome and athletic as all Alphas are expected to be, which can inspire jealousy in others.

He has a tendency to overthink things and often takes the initiative. He knows that he is different from other people and searches in vain for a way to fill the void he feels. He does not know how to share his intelligence and feels that he is wasting it by not using it constructively. He is good-natured and forgives easily.

Watson helps John to fight off the Deltas who try to arrest him at the hospital. Many of his decisions are influenced by his love of literature: for example, he chooses the Falkland Islands as his destination when he is sentenced to exile because he believes that the climate is more suitable for writing than the other potential locations.

LENINA CROWE

Lenina is a Beta-Plus nurse who works in the Fertilizing Room. She is free-spirited and very pretty, and is frequently described as "pneumatic" (a term meaning physically perfect with a well-proportioned body), meaning that men are frequently drawn to her and women often seek her friendship. At the start of the novel, she is set apart by her attachment to Henry Foster, the handsomest man in the Centre, even though romantic affection is strictly prohibited in this "perfect" world. Although she recognises some of the shortcomings of the "brave new world", she has no desire to rebel against the system. Instead, she convinces herself that it works for the greater good and that it deserves to be respected, even though she does not follow all of its rules.

Lenina admires a number of powerful men: she likes Henry Foster because of his attractiveness and scientific expertise, she is attracted to Bernard Marx, who awakens her curiosity, and she is drawn to John because of his different, liberated upbringing. In Chapter 11, her feelings for John are shown to be genuine, so when she is led to believe that he is immune to her charms her pride is deeply wounded. Following this, she is plagued by melancholy and her newfound obsession with John even drives her to spurn Foster. She has no concept of monogamy or fidelity, and since these are core values for John, she is unable to seduce him. The rift between them deepens when John sees her join the crowds of curious spectators around his lighthouse, accompanied by Henry, and verbally lashes out at her.

JOHN

John has no surname because he grew up outside the bounds of civilisation. He was born in the Reservation, and is the son of his Beta mother and the DHC. John is very handsome, received a good education and speaks English. He is even familiar with the works of William Shakespeare (English playwright, 1564-1616), which he quotes often. Unlike the education system of the World State, John chiefly learns from his life experiences, which allows him to analyse things objectively and to become aware of the total lack of freedom that characterises this society.

He is eager to prove himself, and hopes to undertake a rite of passage (Chapter 7). However, he does not have the right to do so because of his complexion and his origins, so these hopes are dashed. He is so shy that he cannot bear to look at Lenina when he is talking to her, even though he is madly in love with her. Since he views sexual desire as a taboo, he expresses his love through poetry and by idealising her. He has a strong bond with nature and soon feels trapped in the new world he is plunged into, which he finds to be lacking in both freedom and authenticity. He is particularly troubled by people's indifference towards death. He puts great stock in the values of honesty and self-respect, and he feels guilty for leaving the Reservation and for having "sold himself" to experience civilisation. At the end of the novel, he mutilates and martyrs himself and eventually dies.

LINDA

Linda is John's mother, and conceived him naturally. She is described as ugly, as she is large, blonde, toothless and dirty. She has a haggard, wrinkled face marked with red veins. She appears to be extremely old.

She misses being a civilised woman, when she was a Beta-Minus worker in the "brave new world". She tells her new friends that she found it very difficult to adjust to the dirt, jealousy and poor living conditions of the Reservation. She has lost all hope, and drowns her sorrows in alcohol since, by her own admission, she could never get used to the customs of her new home. Her alcoholism and *soma* addiction, which are her only ways of escaping reality, eventually lead to her death in a hospital bed with her son at her side.

HENRY FOSTER

Henry is a researcher at the Hatchery and Conditioning Centre. He is a handsome man, with blonde hair and bright blue eyes. Although he is and Alpha and is very sure of himself, he tends to speak very quickly, which can make him seem anxious.

He suppresses all trace of his feelings for Lenina, even though they are regular sexual partners at the beginning of the novel. He has a mischievous streak, and likes to annoy Bernard Marx and mock his grumpiness. He is quite energetic and seems truly passionate about his work, which he discusses with anyone who will listen. He has an answer for everything, and is very educated and a little proud.

MUSTAPHA MOND

Mustapha is a very high-ranking member of society: as the Resident World Controller of

Western Europe, he is one of the ten World Controllers. At the start of the novel, Mustapha seems to be obsessed with keeping society running smoothly, but he shows more tolerance in the final chapters. When he was threatened with exile in his younger years, he chose to give up his passion for science and accept a position of responsibility to avoid being banished. Mond is highly educated and has a very curious mind. He has read widely and has watched a lot of old films, which have instilled the open-mindedness that most other citizens lack in him.

ANALYSIS

UTOPIA AND DYSTOPIA IN LITERATURE

The term *utopia* (Greek for "nowhere") was coined in 1516 by Thomas More (English philosopher, 1478-1535). In his eponymous novel, he described the country of Utopia as a paradise characterised by social integration and the fair distribution of labour. People would coexist in total harmony in this world, where there would be no gods, masters or social divisions.

This concept, which was originally based on the ideas of Plato (Greek philosopher, 427-348/347 BCE) and Aristotle (Greek philosopher, 384-322 BCE), was revisited by 20th-century intellectuals, who then developed the concept of its antithesis, namely the dystopia. In *Brave New World*, Huxley's goal was to use a dystopian setting to illustrate and criticise the way a society which seems to simply be perfectly organised can easily become a dictatorship.

PLATO'S UTOPIA

In the *Republic* (c. 380 BCE), Plato draws on Socratic thought regarding constitutions to outline the possible existence of a perfect society in which people would coexist in perfect harmony. In the essay, Plato discusses the conditions that would need to be satisfied for such a place to exist, and stipulates that the leaders of this society should be philosophers to ensure that it is governed by reason and not emotion. However, Plato also recognises that a society which has been built on reason is not necessarily a utopia.

Although *Brave New World* is often described as a visionary book, Huxley stated that it was never his intention to predict the future; he simply wanted to write about the dictatorships that he believed would eventually come into being. In his opinion, it was only reasonable to assume that, sooner or later, the elite would take control of society and subjugate their fellow citizens by means of psychological terror or pharmaceutical drugs. Huxley believed that entertainment and drugs could be used to condition people into accepting slavery and manipulation, shaping them into mere tools in the hands of society's elite.

THE THREAT OF TECHNOLOGY AND SOCIAL CONDITIONING

Darwinism and eugenics

According to the theories of Charles Darwin (British naturalist, 1809-1882), there are two types of people: the strong and the weak. The first group demonstrates resourcefulness and can survive in this world, while the weaker group tends to disappear. This is called "natural selection".

Eugenics, unlike Darwinism, advocates actively controlling the weaker category. This would involve eliminating their shortcomings, "improving" them and then reintroducing them into society. In the past, eugenics has been used by some totalitarian regimes with the aim of "improving" their populations (for example, Hitler attempted to create a "perfect" Aryan race). This doctrine has developed in tandem with science and technology through the 20th and 21st centuries, and nowadays it is frequently brought up in major debates over subjects such as abortion, euthanasia, overpopulation, aggressive therapy and birth defects.

Eugenics in *Brave New World*

In practice, eugenics involves changing an individual's genetic makeup in the pursuit of a specific result. In *Brave New World*, scientists use this technique on every individual immediately after their conception, and modify their genes to make their physical and mental qualities align with the social class they have been designated for.

There is only one place where children are still conceived naturally: the Reservation, which is considered a savage area and is heavily stigmatised. This preconception goes unchallenged until John, who was born in the Reservation but has been brought up with the customs of the civilised world, breaks down the barriers between these two worlds.

This kind of large-scale eugenics is a complex issue: for example, the citizens of this society completely accept their fate, but this acceptance does not bring them happiness. Instead, they attempt to overcome the drudgery of their lives by indulging in expensive leisure pursuits and drugs, but are unable to truly find a means of escaping reality. Huxley therefore criticises eugenics by demonstrating how it leads to social segregation and division.

Entertainment and happiness

In *Brave New World*, everyone lives peaceful but unfeeling lives in a World State inspired by Fordism, a system aiming to increase productivity which was developed by the American businessman Henry Ford (1863-1947). In this society, all emotions are controlled: familial bonds and passion are proscribed, as are the concepts of monogamy and romantic love.

HENRY FORD AND FORDISM

Henry Ford was born in Michigan, where he embarked on a career as an apprentice mechanic. He built his first automobile model in 1896, and went on to work with Thomas Edison (American inventor and businessman, 1847-1931). In the early 20th century, he and his friends built a racing car, and its commercial success provided him with the necessary funds to found his own business.

He also developed Fordism, a model for labour distribution which is based on a number of key elements: the production line, whereby work is broken down into a number of steps; mass production; and higher salaries for the workers to prevent them from quitting. Everything should also be automated and strictly managed to optimise consumption. The social system of the World State follows a similar logic: social classes are structured in a way that maximises the size of the workforce, and everyone is assigned a specific position to ensure that all work is completed automatically and efficiently. On the other hand, the workers' leisure options and job satisfaction are extremely limited.

However, there are two characters who rebel against this "ideal":

- Bernard Marx is in favour of monogamous relationships, and he believes that happiness can be found by experiencing intense passion and by withdrawing from the overly modern world around him (see Chapter 6).

- John believes that happiness is synonymous with freedom. He longs for simple entertainment which does not rely on new technology, and wants to be able to feel love which is not limited by the constraints imposed by society.

Furthermore, culture has been abolished to make way for expensive leisure activities that encourage people to acquire even more goods; in other words, all entertainment must be economically profitable.

Consumer society and globalisation

Huxley uses the novel to criticise the consumption and overconsumption that has characterised our society since the Industrial Revolution.

THE INDUSTRIAL REVOLUTION AND TAYLORISM

The Industrial Revolution was a period of extremely rapid technological and industrial development which took place in Europe and North America between approximately 1800 and 1930. During this time, the production levels of a number of industrial sectors, such as metallurgy and automobile production, were significantly increased through the application of Taylorism.

This organisational system, which was named after the American engineer Frederick Winslow Taylor (1856-1915), involved dividing the workload into separate tasks which were then assigned to different workers. These workers soon mastered this particular task and began working more quickly, increasing overall efficiency and production levels.

The society in *Brave New World* seems to be based on the principles of Taylorism: work is evaluated, assigned to a class and divided between the workers in each class. From birth, children are conditioned to develop a need to consume in order to ensure that the economy always stays afloat. This deeply rooted desire for material goods means that demand creates supply, not the other way around.

Huxley also addresses the issue of globalisation by setting the novel in a World State that is headquartered in London. All nations have been merged into one, which offers one undeniable advantage: it is impossible for this country to go to war with any other country. On the other hand, the world is governed by a handful of dictatorial men whose power is absolute.

A BRAVE NEW REALITY?

Although Huxley's intention was to write about a society that could potentially become a reality in the very distant future, just 25 years later he was forced to face the uncomfortable truth that the world he had described in the novel bore an uncomfortable degree of resemblance to the society he was living in. This "brave new world" had come into being much more quickly than expected, as he discusses in *Brave New World Revisited*, a reflection on the novel which was published in 1958:

> "In the West, it is true, individual men and women still enjoy a large measure of freedom. But even in those countries that have a tradition of democratic government, this freedom and

> even the desire for this freedom seem to be on
> the wane. In the rest of the world freedom for
> individuals has already gone, or is manifestly
> about to go." (Huxley, 2004: 4)

Of course, western society in 1958 was not exactly identical to the society described in the novel, even though the world had certainly changed a great deal in the years since the novel's publication. However, Huxley believed that the world was more likely to eventually resemble the world he had imagined in his novel than the vision of civilisation that Orwell had presented in *1984*, although he conceded that the latter may have seemed plausible at the time of writing. The key difference between the two novels is fear: Orwell's world is built on the fear of punishment, whereas this element is practically nonexistent in Huxley's work. Overall, the totalitarianism on *1984* is much more repressive, whereas it is more insidious and subtle in *Brave New World*, though no less powerful.

In *Brave New World*, individuals ostensibly have total freedom to love and amuse themselves as they please, but this policy has actually been implemented to make the population easier to manipulate. Although everyone is free to choose who to sleep with, monogamous relationships are prohibited, and their entertainment options are limited to a selection of collective leisure activities which are controlled by the regime or taking *soma*.

In the real world during this time period, technology was advancing in leaps and bounds, with developments including the invention of automated production lines, new methods of transport which made it possible to travel long distances much more quickly, and media such as television, radio and the cinema. In theory, all of these technological advances were for the benefit of the individual, but they actually gave rise to a more tightly regulated society in which it was far easier to spy on its citizens in a manner reminiscent of the all-powerful Big Brother in *1984*. The key difference was that this surveillance was so surreptitious that it went unnoticed, allowing citizens to continue living in relative peace and unconcern.

In *Brave New World Revisited*, Huxley examines the ways that society in 1958 had developed similarities with the society he envisioned in his novel, and sheds new light on the world he imagined. Although it is presented as a flawed but far-off utopia in the novel, it seems a much more plausible and attainable reality in the present day. Only a few technological advances would be necessary for our society to develop several of the most important characteristics of the society depicted in *Brave New World*:

- a dehumanised, passive population who are denied the possibility of happiness because their everyday lives are too monotonous and rigorously organised (in *Brave New World*, individuals are only capable of feeling fulfilled when they use drugs);
- social conditioning which teaches individuals not to question the status quo, which consists of hierarchical social classes.

Huxley did not believe that genetic uniformity could be imposed on society through embryonic manipulation (although more recent scientific discoveries seem to disprove this belief), and he therefore paid more attention to the concept of mental conformity in his work. Similarly, his use of a form of totalitarianism which keeps the population's morale up and incorporates social classes was due to his belief that this approach was most viable.

In his 1958 essay, Huxley also condemned the idea of a deceptively totalitarian system which appears to be above reproach until examined more closely, and emphasised that the fears and questions provoked by the original novel had not been dispelled in the meantime; on the contrary, they were more relevant than ever before. Humanity's dependence on technology was at an all-time high, and essential values like truth and ethics were being sacrificed for the sake of progress. Similarly, the society of *Brave New World* aimed to create a utopian totalitarian state using strict control and increased consumption, and was willing to sacrifice key tenets of civilisation such as family life to achieve these goals. In his essay, Huxley made his opinion very clear: that society was becoming more deeply mired in the errors he had written about in 1932. He also stated that he believed education and work were the keys to reclaiming people's freedom, rather than interpersonal relationships.

FREEDOM IN PERIL

In *Brave New World Revisited*, Huxley wrote "liberty arises and has meaning only within a self-regulating community of freely co-operating individuals" (2004: 30). This could be considered applicable to the society depicted in *Brave New World*, given that the characters are conditioned to feel satisfied with their lives and to believe that the society they are living in is structured to benefit everyone.

However, the flaws in this system quickly become apparent. Each individual's physical appearance and personality are strictly controlled from conception, and during their lives they are subjected to a set of rules which are ostensibly designed to improve their lives, but which actually prevent them from pursuing their deepest desires. For example, Lenina has a long-term relationship with Foster, which violates the ban on monogamy and romantic attachments, and then develops strong (and reciprocated) feelings for John.

When the novel's characters become aware of this discrepancy, they turn away from society to such an extent that they usually end up as outcasts from it:

- Marx and Watson are exiled to far-flung locations under the pretext that their true personalities will have the chance to flourish there;
- John finds it so impossible to find peace in a world so different from the one he grew up in that he eventually turns to self-harm and suicide as a way out.

These fates are symbolic, as they reflect the way that the all-powerful system depicted in *Brave New World* excludes anyone who does not conform to its rules. Huxley feared that this world could someday become a reality.

FURTHER REFLECTION

SOME QUESTIONS TO THINK ABOUT...

- What common feelings and behaviours are forbidden in the society of *Brave New World*? Why?
- What similarities can be found between our society and the society of *Brave New World*? Explain your answer.
- Given the advances that have been made in the field of genetic manipulation, could Huxley's vision become a reality one day? Explain your answer.
- Another famous 20th-century dystopian novel, George Orwell's *1984*, also imagines what England might be like in the future. However, the totalitarian societies described by the two novels are very different. In what ways? Explain your answer.
- In *Brave New World*, society is divided into different classes, which correspond to genetically predetermined physical and intellectual

abilities. In such a system, the upper classes are the most privileged, and the lower classes have the most reason to rebel. Why do they fail to act? Explain your answer.

- Are there any real-life equivalents of *soma* in our world? What are they?
- Imagine what life would be like for Bernard Marx in Iceland.
- In your opinion, was Huxley writing a purely fictional narrative or was he predicting what life would be like in the future? Justify your answer.
- How would you define the concept of freedom in *Brave New World*?
- What kind of rationale governs consumption in the novel? Does it serve a greater purpose?

We want to hear from you!
Leave a comment on your online library
and share your favourite books on social media!

FURTHER READING

REFERENCE EDITION

- Huxley, A. (2007) *Brave New World*. London: Vintage.

REFERENCE STUDIES

- Debaeker, A.-L. (2015) Le «meilleur des mondes», c'est maintenant? *Le Figaro*. [Online]. [Accessed 29 March 2018]. Available from: <http://www.lefigaro.fr/vox/culture/2015/04/17/31006-20150417ARTFIG00267-le-meilleur-des-mondes-c-est-maintenant.php>

- Encylopédie de L'Agora. (2012) *Mondialisation*. [Online]. [Accessed 29 March 2018]. Available from: <http://agora.qc.ca/mot.nsf/Dossiers/Mondialisation>

- Gaulon, J.-F. (2012) Une semaine avec... *Le meilleur des mondes* d'Aldous Huxley. *Agoravox*. [Online]. [Accessed 29 March 2018]. Available from: <https://www.agoravox.fr/culture-loisirs/culture/article/une-semaine-avec-le-meilleur-des-109049>

- HenryFord.fr. (No date) *Fordism*. [Online]. [Accessed 29 March 2018]. Available from: <https://www.henryford.fr/fordisme>

- Huxley, A. (2004) *Brave New World Revisited*. London: Vintage.

- Lefèvre, T. (1997) *La Connexion eugéniste, petite histoire de la culture de la mort*. Nanterre: TDD.

- Romeri, L. (2008) L'imaginaire utopique dans le monde grec, la cité idéale de Platon : de l'imaginaire à l'irréalisable. *Kentron*. [Online]. [Accessed 29 March 2018]. Available from: <https://journals.openedition.org/kentron/1594>

- Roumégoux, C. (2010) Dissertation rédigée sur *Le Meilleur des mondes* d'Aldous Huxley. *WebLettres*. [Online]. [Accessed 29 March 2018]. Available from: <http://www.weblettres.net/blogs/article.php?w=MonplaisirLett&e_id=28257>

- Songes Littéraires. (2009) *Aldous Huxley: faire aimer à la population sa propre servitude*. [Online]. [Accessed 29 March 2018]. Available from: <http://songes-litteraires.over-blog.com/article-le-meilleur-des-mondes-de-aldous-huxley-26499682.html>

- Traineau, B. (No date) La République de Platon. *Une histoire de l'utopie*. [Online]. [Accessed 29 March 2018]. Available from: <http://une-histoire-de-lutopie.edel.univ-poitiers.fr/exhibits/show/sources/sources-antiques/la-r--publique-de-platon>

- Vaugirard, C. (2013) Aldous Huxley, 50 ans après. *Cahiers libres*. [Online]. [Accessed 29 March 2018].

Available from: <http://cahierslibres.fr/2013/11/
aldous-huxley-50-ans-apres>

ADAPTATIONS

- *Brave New World*. (1980) [Television film]. Burt
  Brinckerhoff. Dir. USA: Universal Television.
- *Brave New World*. (1998) [Television film]. Leslie
  Libman and Larry Williams. Dir. USA: NBC.

www.brightsummaries.com

Ebook EAN: 9782806270337

Paperback EAN: 9782806272607

Legal Deposit: D/2015/12603/564

This guide was written with the collaboration of
Lucile Lhoste and translated with the collaboration
of Emma Hanna for the sections "Eugenics in *Brave
New World*", "A brave new reality?" and "Freedom
in peril", as well as the boxes "Plato's utopia" and
"Henry Ford and Fordism".

Cover: © Primento

Digital conception by Primento, the digital partner of
publishers.

Made in the USA
Las Vegas, NV
28 June 2021